Strengthening Local NGOs Internal Capacity: Experiences from the Field

Rehema C Batti

First Printing: 2015

ISBN #:978-1-329-08638-8

Dedication

This book is dedicated to Dr Samoel Khamadi,
Natasha, Hope, and Zawadi
who are a constant source of inspiration.

Aknowledgements

With special thanks to my husband, Dr S. Khamadi and children Natasha, Hope and Zawadi for all your love, prayers and support. You have been my inspiration and motivation for continuing to move my career forward. Thanks for not just believing, but knowing that I could do this!

I would like to thank my parents Karissa and Rachel Batti for encouraging me to follow my dreams and their support throughout my career. To my siblings Steve, George, Masika, and Riziki thanks for the encouragement that you provide each one of you in your own special ways.

Table of Contents

Preface

In many African nations, local NGOs are growing yet sometimes their organizational management structures and practices are not adequate to support sustainable delivery of quality services.

Capacity building has been a challenge in many countries in the African continent. This is because capacity-building interventions undertaken in LNGOs have failed to produce sustainable changes within the organizations.

Currently, most capacity development efforts focus on providing support in the area of staff technical competencies with minimal or no support given to strengthening the internal management or governance systems of the organization.

An organization that is managed well is crucial as it increases the chances of gaining diverse stakeholder support and resources. In my working experience with Non-Governmental organizations (NGOs), I have noted there is a great need for strengthening management and governance systems in these organizations in addition to technical support currently provided.

Many local organizations fail to get funds or resources for many various reasons, but one critical reason is that they have inadequate or lack stable internal management systems to support program interventions or ensure the sustainability of the organizations.

Local NGOs need to plan for their future and have the relevant internal management and leadership structures that ensure sustainability and improve overall performance.

The solution to this is to embrace organization development (OD) as a key catalyst for organizational growth. The aim of this book is to stir up among NGO staff and students undertaking community development and capacity building practitioners an appreciation for OD.

OD (Organizational Development) is the missing link in the current efforts of providing a holistic approach to capacity building efforts. The book highlights challenges that act as barriers to embracing OD interventions among local NGOs and highlights good practices that can be adopted by stakeholders or agencies who seek to introduce OD as a strategy to support organizations they work with.

This book will be a useful resource for local NGO leadership and management in their pursuit to develop sustainable organizations in resource-constrained environments. The insights shared in this book aim to advocate for a nurturing relationship that is based on respect and understanding of the challenges that exist when undertaking OD interventions among local NGOs.

Introduction

Collaboration with local NGOs has become an important feature in the development sector. Local NGOs bring the advantage of being indigenous organizations with close links to communities they serve.

There is a need to understand that, not all local NGOs move forward consistently in their growth and no organization comes into existence fully mature with all capacities in place. Some organizations regress depending on internal or external factors that affect them for example departure of a leader or discontinuation of funding, or change of policies within the country.

NGOs face multiple issues in the area of credibility and competence. There are other challenges that affect NGOs in many African countries in relation to governance and leadership, financial management, program development, logistics, human resource management, communication, public relations, and marketing.

Therefore, there is an increasing need to use OD interventions to assist local NGO improve their internal structures which have an impact on how they relate to both the internal and external environment. There are now emerging new approaches and efforts by aid agencies to strengthen NGO capacity and performance. However the success of these organizations is largely dependent on the governance and management systems in place.

Clear, accountable structures and systems are essential for the development of a successful and credible NGO. Local NGOs should anticipate growth and reorganize their organizations through equipping them with fundamental management systems and structures.

Batti[i] observes that proper management and governance structures should form the backbone of organizations that desire to grow towards sustainability.

The approach of capacity building in the development sector has risen to address the challenges of unequal relationship and barriers to sustainability between international and local NGOs engagements.

Organizational development is a crucial process that strengthens key organizational dimensions and is relevant in NGO growth and management. An essential requirement for an effective OD approach is whereby both parties, those providing and receiving the support understand their contribution to the successful implementation of interventions.

Therefore, it is important to have a more proactive approach in developing and building sustainable NGOs through planning and budgeting for relevant Organizational Development (OD) interventions.

Batti [ii] describes organizational development as a management practice that applies relevant knowledge areas, information, technologies, and other measures to improve processes of organizational change.

Despite NGOs having knowledge on good OD practices in reality, they face significant challenges in translating OD principles into good practice.

Organizations that desire to serve society better and be relevant for their role need to question continuously the relevance and position of their programs' efficiency, effectiveness, impact, and sustainability.

Organizations must be able to question the reason for any "problems" occurring, evaluate their programs and self evaluate the organization itself. This is one of the local NGOs greatest weak point, and despite the clear desire for service to and transform communities, local NGOs struggle to change so that they can be better equipped to provide support.

Woodman, Pasmore and Shani,[iii] note that organizations that fail to learn from errors become vulnerable to predictable 'surprises.' Organizations need to embrace change to become effective in achieving their organizational mandates and to satisfy diverse stakeholders' expectations on project results.

Change is required at organizational level because technologies are rapidly evolving and stakeholders' demands on supporting sustainable projects have increased. Organizations should therefore strive to develop and focus on new strategies that build organizational internal management structures and processes.

Change is also required of individuals who make up the organizations through learning and adopting new skills because of job changes, redesign, or elimination. If organizations wish to increase their influence, provide quality service to communities', and effectively fulfill their mandates, they must be able to question the reason for lack of organization growth or poor performance.

Organizations need to have a real ability for self-evaluation. An organization is seen to have the capacity to sustain itself if it has a vision, strategy, composition, culture, competence, and capital to enable it undertake its mission. Some of these capacity elements are visible and other invisible and for an organization to be effective, it is required to gradually develop and maintain a balance of these factors in the life of the organization.

Organizations are made up of individuals who bring with them personalities, values, visions, and inadequacies that may influence an organization's systems and at the same time, the organization shapes the individuals and relations within. The OD process provides NGOs an opportunity to develop consistently through understanding the complex interactions involved within an organization as a system.

NGOs that are effective are fundamental for promoting developmental change that is transformational. This change has lasting positive impacts on the lives of communities, particularly the most vulnerable.

Chapter One: Capacity Development Practice

To understand how organization development practice is implemented. We will first explore the common and widely used concept of capacity building or capacity development. This is the entry point for the concept and practice of OD especially with stakeholders who support local NGOs.

Capacity is defined as the potential of individuals or organizations to function efficiently. An NGO has to have the ability to influence its environment and accept that it has a responsibility for the social and political environment surrounding it.

As NGOs have continued to grow in scale, they have realized limits to their effectiveness. They now face the pressure of examining their organization management issues in more detail if they are to attract aid funding.

Organizations have realized they need strong organizational structures if they are to make continuous impact in the development sector, to receive funding and recognition at national level.

Overview of Capacity Development Dimensions and Components

What is capacity development

The term capacity development is used sometimes interchangeably with the word capacity building. It is a development approach that focuses on identifying barriers that inhibit individuals, institutions, NGOs, and governments from achieving their objectives and building their abilities to do so.

Capacity building efforts recognize that organizations need a set of core capabilities which they can adopt and implement to become more sustainable. The purpose of capacity-building is to enable an entity to be self reliant and productive as they implement and serve communities.

Capacity development attempts to strengthen interaction between an organization and its environment. It is deemed effective, when it gradually builds the capacity of an NGO's ability to undertake its goals over time, and enhances its ability to have a transformational impact among communities served.

Currently grant making bodies and international development agencies recognize the need for capacity development of NGOs. It rests on the principle that investing in organizations and individuals enables them develop capacities needed for them to thrive and achieve development objectives.

The concept and practice of capacity building developed from (1950s) as institutional building approach, (1970s-1980s) as human development approach and (2000s) as capacity development.

However, it is crucial to adopt a participatory approach in capacity building that ensures development efforts are sustainable and develop into empowering partnerships for which there is a high degree of ownership.

Different perspectives are used to define and engage in capacity building interventions.Blumenthal[iv] ,highlights three perspectives or approaches

i.   A capacity-building program that is defined as an effort to help non-profits through a particular approach that is defined in grant making guidelines.

ii.   A capacity-building grant provides support to a single organization to undertake capacity-building activities.

iii. A capacity building engagement refers to a specific capacity building effort within a single organization. For example, a single grant may support both a strategic planning process and the installation of new accounting software.

Ubels, Naa-Aku, and Fowler[v] note that openness and complexity are two characteristics of organization functioning and process that bring about change towards greater effectiveness.

Ubels, Naa-Aku, and Fowler[vi] further highlight the following elements required within organizations for one to ascertain that capacity is within or developing in an organization

i.   An organization has the ability to do.

ii.   An organization has the ability to act and self organize

iii. An organization has ability to generate development results

iv.   An organization has ability to relate

v.   An organization has ability to adapt and self-renew

vi.   An organization has ability to achieve coherence

The capacity of an organization according to Ubels, Naa-Aku, and Fowler[vii] is shaped by, adapts to, and reacts to both external and internal factors. It includes skills, systems, processes, and ability to relate to others.

Thus, capacity development is a change process that modifies some of these factors. Organizations and people have either strong or weak desire to change, develop, and learn due to their environment or internal factors. Capacity development (CD) takes place within people and organizations, and it cannot be forced upon them.

Ubels, Naa-Aku, and Fowler,[viii] observe that for NGO participation to grow in service delivery they need to be effective. Capacity development can help improve an organization's effectiveness in relation to its objectives and context.

Capacity development of institutions (NGOs) embraces the following components and goes beyond training to include:

i.   Human resource development-(equipping individuals with skills, knowledge and information

ii. Organizational development -(focus on internal management structures and procedures within organizations.

iii. Institutional development-(focus on regulatory external aspects to enable organizations operate within a conducive environment)

Therefore, an adequate organization capacity building approach:

i.   Improves the overall function of an entity.

ii.   Interventions target the entire organization and system

iii. Involvement of individuals who are in charge of their learning

iv.   Purpose is to facilitate organizational change

v.   It is multi-disciplinary and uses a variety of tools and mechanisms

According to Batti,[ix] effective capacity building involves considering the whole organization and taking the systems view of any interventions. It is important to avoid subjecting NGOs to interventions that may undo or undermine other capacity building efforts.

However very few organizations are fortunate to receive capacity building with a focus on internal organization component, and this has hindered the growth and stability of many organizations. Many donors perceive that embarking on OD support among NGOs is too expensive a venture to engage in, and hence they end up focusing only on the staff project technical aspect of capacity building.

Donor agencies and other stakeholders continue to focus on the human capacity development and the policy environment but minimal or no effort is made to deliberately target and build the internal organizational structures or capacity. This has resulted in the death, closure, or decline of development projects or the local organizations themselves.

The Capacity Development Process

Capacity development (CD) is seen as an ongoing process that is planned and organization- wide. It seeks to optimize an organization's operation in relation to its objectives, funds, and environment.

Before any CD intervention is done, an assessment is conducted to identify capacity gaps. Capacity building at whatever level needs to consider both the institutional and organizational context. It should be driven by a clear focus on the desired outcome which is "what are we trying to achieve at the end?"

The capacity building process involves the following steps;

i) Entry phase

This stage involves gathering of information on the size of the organization, its strategy, staffing, getting buy-in from management, and understanding the purpose of initiating a capacity development process.

ii) Assessment phase

It involves a series of analysis using developed tools and approaches. Mostly assessments are conducted to identify the strengths and gaps facing the organizations.

Organizations in this stage ask the following:

a. Is what we are already doing restricting us from doing things more effectively?

b. Are there other ways we can adopt to achieve better results?

c. Are there things we are already doing well that we need to continue with or revise?

iii) Planning and designing phase

In this stage options are discussed and prioritized that will address the gaps or areas of concern identified. Time- lines and expected outcomes are indicated.

iv) Implementation and monitoring phase

The agreed interventions are undertaken, and progress measured at periodic intervals as indicated in the plan.

v) Review and re-plan phase

The plan is reviewed and the outcomes achieved are evaluated against what was intended. During this stage, the team will re-plan if objectives were not achieved or not delivering expected results.

vi) Transition phase

Once the intended outcome of the capacity development initiative is achieved, this will lead to the end of the CD support. However, in some situations where it is observed that no changes are likely to take place despite the efforts being put then the CD support is terminated. The CD process is cyclic in nature, and the assessment of the current and desired state is the beginning of any capacity development process within an organization.

In many a practice, what is often seen is a direct implementation of a capacity building approach that uses a top-bottom approach with no feedback or review of what currently exists. This has lead to many capacity-building efforts not yielding favorable results.

Sahley [x] identifies three groups of NGO capacities:

(a) Identity, culture and purpose, such as the capacity for an explicit ideology of development, good staff/management relations and effective conflict resolution mechanisms;

(b) Management systems and structure this means an NGO has clear procedures, roles and responsibilities, effective decision- making and financial management structures;

(c) Programme and technical capacity, which refers to the ability of the NGO to deliver services effectively and develop strategies based on understanding social, political, and economic context.

According to Blumenthal,[xi] there exist four key elements that play an important role in dictating the scope, design, and ultimate success of any capacity building engagement:

    i.   The desired outcome or defining goal;

    ii.   The change strategy selected to help realize that goal;

    iii.   The champions guiding the efforts, be they internal or external;

    iv.   The resources—time, energy and money—invested in the process.

Blumenthal [xii] further argues that most capacity-building approaches adopted by organizations are either a focus, problem-centered approach or a broader commitment to work on a range of organizational issues.

In most cases, direct response capacity building programs are problem-centered and capacity-building initiatives take a broader approach to organizational development.

According to Woodman, Pasmore, and Shani,[xiii]the process of developing and sustaining effectiveness is extremely challenging.

Therefore, when capacity building is identified as the approach to improve organizational effectiveness, it would be prudent to emphasize also improving internal management systems and organizational structure.

Overview of Organizational Sustainability

The involvement of NGO in development has become more demanding and organizations are seen to suffer from the consequences of under-investment in basic organizational functions and practices.

NGOs sometimes lack the capacity to adapt and take on new functions, and this is often linked to weak internal organization structures. Many local NGOs (LNGOs) face the challenge of sustainability and especially those in under-resourced and remote areas.

Sustainability has become an important issue, and it is crucial to any organization's success and continued performance. Many LNGOs, however, are still trying to grapple with how to embed sustainability into their organizational culture.

Components of Organizational Sustainability

Organization sustainability is a journey and not a state. A sustainable organization must meet the needs and expectations of society and its stakeholders while still putting emphasis on financial and social management aspects.

Definition:

Sustainability is defined, as the capability of an entity to mobilize and oversee resources to support it fulfill its mandate consistently over a period without excessive overreliance on a single funding mechanism.

It may also mean the capacity of an organization to provide quality services continually and achieve results long after external funding ends.Organization sustainability is an ongoing process and resembles a plant. The following is a summary of three components of sustainability:

a) Institutional sustainability

A sustainable organization has a missión and a strategic plan that is linked to missión and visión. The organization has an annual process that links annual plans and budgets to a strategic plan.

A sustainable organization needs to be proactive and flexible. This is because there are changes that occur either externally or internally within an organization's surrounding environment.

b) Financial sustainability

It is what drives the institutional motor and an organization that lacks finances cannot hire staff or procure goods and services.

An organization needs to be aware of resources needed to support its activities and will most often than not require resources from other external sources.

c) Moral sustainability

An organization needs a clear mission and leadership commitment to its overall vision. Staff commitment to the organization's mandate is rewarded in diverse ways that are motivating.

The leadership, management, and staff act ethically, and there is no room for engaging in unlawful actions. An organization cannot exist for a long time with unethical and questionable practices.

Unethical practices often cause damage to an organization's reputation beyond their ability to control. This is something that happens in reality and has resulted in some local NGOs losing funding because of moral and ethical issues.

No donor or stakeholder wants to work with an organization that is not credible. Therefore achieving sustainability is an ongoing process and not a single step or initiative.

Sustainable organizations are not necessarily self-sufficient entities but can be financially self-reliant. Sustainability in simple terms can be described as continuity. For an organization to be sustainable, it needs to be strong financially, morally and institutionally.

Unfortunately, an extraordinary performance in one area cannot conceal the weakness in the other areas. Hence, effective management and growth of the three components is crucial if an organization is to be sustainable.

Any CD or OD intervention should, therefore, strive to ensure that sustainability is the key strategic priority during implementation. Organizations can further incorporate sustainability by engaging in inter-organizational collaborations, include sustainability aspects in their strategic planning process, and change their business approaches or models based on the context of their operating environment.

Chapter Two: Organization Development Concept and Practice

Keeping an organization sustainable requires consistent and continuous targeted efforts to improve an organization's internal operations.

However, many LNGOs are unable to take advantage of their ideas and bring products or services that are acceptable within the market. This occurrence is referred to as the "success trap" which means organizations suffer from "active inertia" or organizational "inertia".

This is scenerio occurs when an organization lacks the internal capacity to exploit external and internal opportunities that exist at a given time. LNGOs need to adopt relevant internal procedures and systems that will support organizational growth and competitiveness.

Woodman, Pasmore and Shani [xiv] observe that companies that were once thriving ten years before were found to have collapsed or closed. This failure of companies shows how even big successful companies face failure.

The very strength that is responsible for success is sometimes the source of rigidities that block the adaptation process. Organization development is a capacity building approach that seeks to engage an organization in continuous improvements based on changing contexts both internally and externally.

Definition and History of Organization Development

An organization is a social unit geared to undertake a specific purpose. It is a system consisting of four interacting subsets; structure, task, technology and people. These subsets are continually changing and as they interact, change is inevitable.

An organization will encounter changes during its lifetime and hence it is important that it evolves if it is to continually achieve its vision and mission.

Definition of Organization Development (OD)

Organization development is a systematic organization-wide process undertaken using targeted intervention to increase an organization's effectiveness.

Organization development is described as a process that aims at increasing organizational effectiveness and advancing individual and organizational change through the application of interventions guided by social and behavioral science knowledge.

Organization Development has emerged into the development platform as part of a renewed interest in capacity development of NGOs. It originated in the USA as a discipline in the 1960s but it is thought to have begun as far as the 1930s.

Organization development seeks to enable an organization effectively achieve its mission and objectives. It provides an opportunity for NGOs to influence operations within both the organization and the environment.

The objective of OD is to

i.   Increase an organizational capacity to problem solve and make changes

ii. Enable an organization put in place processes to improve ongoing internal operations within an organization

iii. Ensure that personnel competencies are effectively utilized

iv. Build a culture of learning from practice

The overall aim of undertaking OD is to make lasting change in the performance and disposition of a whole organization or a unit within an organization.

This means OD interventions target integral aspects of an organization's structure, process, and functioning. Implementation of the interventions, therefore, requires commitment and scrutiny from the leaders and members of the organization for visible changes to the realized.

History of Organizational Development

Organization Development originated from the business world but is now used within other sectors or disciplines globally. It stemmed out of human relations studies during 1930s when psychologists became aware that structures and processes within organizations influenced employee motivation and conduct.

a) Kurt Lewin **(1898-1947)** is the founding father of organization development (OD).He advanced the concept of group dynamics and action research, which are the basis of basic organization development processes. He has contributed to the evolution of OD, as it is known today.

b) **1947**- Research Center for Group Dynamics members were part of the team that founded the national training laboratories from which the T-group and group-based OD emerged and NTL (USA) advanced the research into applied behavioral sciences.

c) **1950s**- During this era saw the emergence of human relations movements, growth of social and developmental psychology and socio-technical systems thinking

d) **During 1967 and 1968**-During these years Likert and Mann pioneered survey feedback to help organization leaders understand the impact they have on people and performance. This was later followed by the creation of T-group Lewin (USA) and Tavistock Insitute developed the unstructured group laboratory training and action learning sets.

e) **1974**-Friendler and Brown researched on organization development (OD) as a method of planned approach to change effort

f) **1980s** - Nielson and Schein supported the idea that OD activities have an impact on social processes within an organization and introduced the general system theory thinking and during this time also the first OD Code of

Ethics was published in the Organization Development institute's monthly newsletter.

g) **1997**- In these years, there was the linking of the application of planned OD interventions within organization and it was seen to contribute to improved organizational effectiveness.

h) **2000s to date**: In this era, OD knowledge and practice continues to be informed by new insights in various disciplines. The use of OD interventions has expanded to focus on aligning organizations through learning.

What Organization Development is Not?

Anderson [xv]describes what organizational development is not:

a) Management consulting

Organizations attempt conscious changes for example implementing changes in organization strategy or direction. OD offers relevant processes to ensure the change occurs as planned and hence goes beyond consulting.

b) Training and development

Capacity development at the individual level is a component of OD yet OD is not confined to training only. It focuses on organization-wide change that may or may not require individuals within the organizations to acquire skills but be guided and coached to use already existing skills to improve the organization functions.

c) Short term

It is a known fact that most changes take long to be realized within organizations. OD, therefore, seeks to provide systemic changes that are long lasting and sustainable and hence cannot be short term.

d) The application of a toolkit

Many times, OD has been perceived as a toolkit. This notion is not correct although OD does occasionally use a toolkit, but it does more than that. It uses multiple strategies and procedures to move an organization from one point to another.

e) Not a mechanism to get funding

Many times OD is seen as a channel for getting funds. Some organizations and donors link OD with the process of funding. OD is a process that provides an organization-wide improvement and not for gaining funding.

Justification for Undertaking Organization Development

The context within the development sector has continued to change as local NGOs become more involved in addressing development issues within different nations.

This has lead to a growing focus on developing and strengthening NGO capacity to enable them manage development projects as partners or collaborators. There are three reasons that justify the need to support and encourage undertaking of OD interventions among organizations.

1. The realities of the aid system and recent changes in the external environment

NGOs have continued to receive resources, which has contributed to them increasing in number, size and scope in countries and fields where they operate. Growth has also increased through government agencies channeling aid resources through NGOs hence their budgets have expanded greatly.

Organizations have now realized operating within an open aid system means a change in one part eventually affects another. This means an organization has to adapt to the changes as well.

This trend continues as funding increases from donor agencies and governments to local NGOs. Secondly, changes in domestic and international priorities of the donor agencies and governments have affected the volume of funds available to organizations. These external changes have created demands on internal organizational and operational structures within NGOs involved in the development sector.

Donors and governments are now demanding to see good governance and management systems within the organization before offering support. This situation has meant that not all NGOs receive funds or resources as expected.

They are required to provide evidence that their organizational structures and systems can support the funding and provide sustainable impacts at grassroot level.

2. Concerns about development impact of NGO interventions

In the recent years, a lot of emphasis has been on ensuring that aid provided produces concrete results and adds value for money. Concerns arising are that NGOs are failing to achieve the sustainable impact that was expected.

There is growing recognition by donor agencies and governments that challenges experienced in programs/projects are linked to internal organizational weakness of the NGOs.

This has led to the push to adopt and undertake OD interventions to improve the organizational structures and systems if funding is to be disbursed to NGOs consistently. This emphasis has pressurized local NGOs to realize the need to strengthen their management capacities if they are to continue to receive funding and be sustainable in the long-run.

3. International regulation standards for aid agencies

The Canadian Council for International Cooperation [xvi] asserts in their Code of Ethics 'that strengthening of people's organizations, voluntary agencies and other socially beneficial institutions is fundamental to the practice of development"

Unfortunately, not all organizations have made the building of partner organization internal organization structure a priority. Some of the impacts related to aid transfers are as follows lack of respect, mistrust, inappropriate salary and benefit structures, competition among aid agencies, hiring staff from local NGOs to work in national NGOs programs have led to weakening rather than strengthening local organizations.

The Organization Lifecycle Components

Organizations are likened to a plant and seen as living systems that are affected by actions within or externally. They start as small entities then expand to huge organizations over a period of time. There can never be two organizations that are similar as organizations grow and develop based on their experiences, context, age and external environment.

To understand and explain the growth of organizations, scholars have identified phases of growth that are likely to be observed in an organization. There are four to five level/stages in any organization.

1. Start up   2. Growth

2. Maturity   4. Decline/Renewal

The process described is not linear but spiral as organizations could be at different phases at different periods. In addition to this, different components within an organization can experience the different stages at different times. This can affect the overall performance or growth within an organization. Other scholars have presented the organizational life cycle phases as follows:

1) <u>Richard Daft</u>

Daft, Willmot, Murphy [xvii] state that there exist four stages in an organizational life cycle that include the following:

1. Entrepreneurial stage   2. Collectivity stage

3. Formalization stage   4. Elaboration stage

2) <u>Griener's Sequential Process</u>

The author outlines how organizations go through a series of stages as they expand and progress. They begin with creativity, direction, delegation, coordination, collaboration, alliances, and finally a discussion.

Characteristics of NGOs in Organization Development Lifecycle Phases

a) Startup stages

i.   Organization objectives are often unclear

ii. Fragile management systems

iii. Founder makes program decisions

iv. Few initiatives without donor support

v.   Income limited or non-existent

vi. Income limited or non-existent

vii. Limited number of staff

viii. Board in formation or does not exist

b) Developing stages

i.   Organization has established functional units

ii. Has some long term goals

iii. Organization chart exists but does not reflect realities

iv. Records& reports are done to satisfy donors

v.   Supervisors do not plan and regularly report

     vi.   Board members are friends or family of founder

     vii.   Community outreach sporadic

     viii.   Increased reliance on external donors

b) <u>Expanding stages</u>

     i.   Board in place and fully functional

     ii.   Strategic and sustainability plans implemented

     iii.   Personnel policies implemented but not consistently followed

     iv.   More sophisticated organogram-shows relationships

     v.   Systems developed, implemented with written guidance

     vi.   Increased diversity of donors, revenue

     vii.   Staff trainings depend on donor support and requirements

     viii.   Community outreach incorporated in project design

     ix.   Management is decentralized

c) <u>Maturity/Renewal stages</u>

     i.   Board participate in resource mobilization and fundraising

ii. Board monitoring the implementation of the strategic plan

iii. Organizational procedure manual exist and cover all organizational aspects and guide operations and decisions.

iv. Staff development and mechanisms in place

v. Above 50% of operations supported by self- generated revenues

vi. Effective human resources, financial management systems in place

vii. Routine review, updating of management systems, training on systems

viii. Ability to track cost centres, project revenues and expenditures

ix. Marketing assets including training to generate revenue

x. Planning process receives input from lower levels (Bottom- up approach) within the organization

d) <u>Decline stages</u>

    i.   Board meetings not done consistently and inconsistent participation(loss of morale and members)

    ii.   Support for operations from self-generated revenues goes to below 15%

    iii.   Loss of credibility with funders and clients

    iv.   Inconsistent program quality

    v.   Organization no longer meeting market needs

    vi.   Decline in product/program quality

    vii.   Organization loses ability to retain staff

    viii. Planning not reflective of the organizational strategic plan

    ix.   Executive Director is inaccessible and unable to keep up with the market/sector changes

There is a relationship between the lifecycle stage of an organization and its effectiveness. The framework above helps organizations to understand themselves better and identify the areas they need to focus on to activate growth. It is crucial to know that different organizations will evolve and develop at different timelines.

Organization Development frameworks

OD is a process of analyzing, action planning and implementation with the purpose of bringing about change within the organization to improve their capacity to implement and manage future changes.

The following section will highlight three frameworks that can be used to help understand how organizations function.

1.   Three Circles Model

The three- circles model has three components. The 'to do' component focuses on the project performance, impact, and effectiveness. The 'to relate' piece focuses on exploring nature of external linkages with other stakeholders.

The 'to be' piece focuses on the inner elements of an organization. The circles interlock to emphasize that a change or a problem with one component will influence the other components. This reinforces the aspect of looking at an organization as a whole, rather than piecemeal.

2. The Onion Model

The model focuses on understanding the surrounding context, which may influence an organization. Focusing for example on the 'to be' component; it is possible to examine organizations a bit deeper using the image of the 'onion-skin'. The external layer of the onion depicts financial and physical resources, which an organization requires.

The layer that follows is staff competencies needed to undertake the tasks. The layer that follows is structures and systems needed to make an organization function. This is followed by the vision, purpose, and strategy of the organization. At the very center of the onion lies its core this represents the identity, values, beliefs, culture and perception of the world.

The outer layers of the 'onion-skin' are elements of capacity that are easily assessed and those nearer to the core are those, which are largely observable only through the impact they have, internally and externally.

The inner central elements are deep rooted and challenging to understand but without 'health' within this component, it will be of no use addressing issues in the outer layers as these are affected by what is depicted at the core.

For example, training of staff will not be productive, if they are not clear about the mission of their organization and this means they will struggle to apply the skills gained due to an organization culture that is closed to learning and application of new skills.

3. Harold Leavitt's System Model

It is also known as the diamond model. Institutional success is impacted by the interaction of task, technology, people, and structure. This model implies that any alteration in one of the area affected the others. Hence, when considering undertaking an OD intervention the four interacting subsets are to be taken into account because, changes in one subset affects the others.

Using the three models, observations, and deductions are made on organizational factors that influence the effective implementation of OD interventions and the overall functioning and performance within the organization.

An organization's motivation to adopt OD interventions to improve capacity is determined by the organization's history, culture, mission, leadership, incentives, and reward system. The effectiveness of OD interventions is measured in terms of improvements observed in the performance of the sub-components where the change has been implemented.

Chapter Three: Organizational Challenges Facing Local NGOs

The management of institutions is crucial and literature shows many local NGOs in African countries have low continuity and sustainability capacity.

OD interventions consist of specific activities designed to effect change in an organization in the long term. These interventions are geared towards improving the entire organization through change. While organizations are unique and each faces its own struggles and success, some common themes can be observed in many local NGOs.

This section will attempt to highlight some obstacles that NGOs face based on field assessments, literature reviews and field observations among various local NGOs. The common gaps observed have been summarized within selected key components listed (*this list is not exhaustive*).

These gaps identified within these components tended to affect the sustainability of local organizations and their performance in undertaking development projects.

Obstacles Faced by Local NGOs

The following are observed obstacles affecting local NGOs in developing countries.

1. Governance structure and process

Governance and leadership are crucial aspects in an organization and they are seen as significant contributors to an organization's performance. One of the greatest challenges facing local NGOs is their governance system. Many local NGOs are observed to have inadequate or weak governance structures despite having board of directors. There still exists a major gap between their adoption and board effectiveness.

Many local NGOs do not have a board because of the complexity of establishing one, and in the recruitment of willing and skilled local people to sit on the board.

For those who are fortunate to have a board it is not uncommon for the director or CEO of the organization to preside over the board. Sometimes the boards are seen to attempt to influence the autonomy of the work of the organization and perhaps even lure the organization towards their individual interests.

Other obstacles noted are lack of a properly constituted board, incomplete documentation of board meetings, board members do not regularly meet or even understand what their role is.

There is minimal involvement by the board members in resource mobilization and vision planning for the organization. In most local NGOs, very few board members exhibit strategic skills or focus. They often tend to interfere with the implementation of programs. The founders of some local NGOs often do not want to adopt more formal structures that are required as a result of an increase in funding and presence of diverse donor resources.

This creates confusion and frustrations among staff within the organization.

Good governance is practiced by having checks and balances that divide control and authority between management and a governing structure to ensure organizational mandates are achieved. However, many local NGO boards fall short in terms of their composition, objectivity, and effectiveness.

2. Organizational Management

Currently NGOs are recognized as development collaborators yet minimal focus is paid to their organization and management capacity. Local NGOs have tended to come rather late into the idea of management. The uncertainty of continuity of donor funding forces NGOs to live a project-to-project existence. This scenario makes it difficult to design and expand the organization in terms of its management structures and systems.

In the past, NGOs have considered it unnecessary to pay serious attention to their internal organizational management capacity, as it was perceived to be taking attention away from their "actual" work. In the end, this results in some organizations having weak management systems and inappropriate organizational processes that are sometimes tied to external funding or an individual (mostly the founders).

In addition, some LNGOs lack clear organo-grams and this has caused conflicts between management and staff roles. The organizations sometimes lack a clear focus on their mission and rely on goals stipulated in projects that are donor funded.

Many local NGOs continue to face the dilemma of handing over management responsibilities to a new person at a very short notice, which causes an imbalance in the organizational structure or system.

This has been due to the local NGOs lacking a "leadership succession plan" which more often than not is considered irrelevant because organizations do not envision their future past the project's funding or founder members.

3. Human Resource capacity and management

People are an important aspect of all social organizations. Batti [xviii] observes that the importance of people is immense as they implement an organization's objectives and achievements for which organizations are recognized.

People are important resources and organizations cannot exist without them. However many local NGOs are small sized or resource constrained and therefore they lack a comprehensive human resource (HR) function or adequate HR competency to recruit and manage qualified staff.

In addition, some local NGOs tend to have inadequate staff numbers in relation to projects implemented while other organizations staff lack relevant experience and skills for their positions. Many local NGOs rely on external funding, therefore recruitment of staff is project based, and the engagement terms are for short durations. This makes it becomes difficult for the organizations to develop staff talent consistently.

Some program managers have inadequate human resource (HR) skills and competencies required to manage staff. They tend to focus more on program priorities hence do not invest adequate time to build their capacity in necessary HR competencies.

Another gap noted is some local NGOs operate without adequate HR guidelines or policies. This affects the recruitment, retention, talent development, and management of human resources within these organizations. Staff turnovers tend to be high in local NGOs and this is attributed partly to inadequate HR management systems and practices.

4. Managing and building external relations

Donor and other partnership challenges are common among local NGOs. Some Local NGOs have weak linkages with other stakeholders or minimal engagement with government departments in their areas of operations.

Others lack a communication or external relations strategy that would help them build their profile among external stakeholders. A lot of competition is seen to prevail among the NGOs and this makes it difficult to work closely with others.

5. Capturing project progress best practices

The need for formal monitoring, evaluation reporting, and learning (MERL) of projects undertaken is becoming a worldwide norm. An efficient monitoring, learning, and evaluation structure is crucial as it enables learning within organizations.

However, many local NGOs face challenges of lacking competency, resources, and tools for tracking and measuring the impact of diverse project activities. This is evident as many local NGOs lack a documented M/E (monitoring and evaluation) framework, inadequate staff capacity in monitoring, reporting, and developing monitoring and evaluation tools.

6. Organizational resources

Sufficient and consistent funding is one of the greatest challenges faced by the institutions and this affects the overall organization performance and sustainability. Development organizations need resources to help them continue providing services to the community.

Donor agencies and governments are keen to search for stable and 'good' NGOs to support. According to Batti[xix] the author observes that in Africa despite vast differences among the local

NGOs, most share a common challenge of unlimited needs chasing limited resources.

Local NGOs face difficulties securing enough funds because of inadequate capacity to mobilize for sufficient resources to undertake projects that normally require substantial amounts of both financial and non-financial resource due to high poverty levels in most parts of the continent. Therefore, many local NGO projects stall or are not undertaken due to inadequate resources.

However, in some countries due to instability issues, local NGOs are sometimes perceived as "enemies" of the state and hence stringent policies are made that make it difficult for local NGOs to easily access resources.

7. Fund management

Many organizations are inadequately resourced and often struggle to make end meets within their organizations. They face stiff competition in accessing funds from external donors.

However, many local NGOs continue to struggle with weak or inadequate finance structures and systems once they receive funding. In addition, the NGOs lack qualified and/or adequate finance staff, have inadequate finance policies and systems, lack clear and informative financial records.

These challenges weaken the organization's capability to manage financial resources accessed from diverse sources and results in many local NGOs losing their financial and non-financial resources, in the end.

Summary:

The majority of challenges observed relate to an organization's operations and management (Process and Structure).When working with local NGOs, this is a common scenerio but unfortunately it is one of the area most neglected when building the capacity of organizations.

Some consequences experienced as a result of the gaps identified:

a) Where there are no organizational policies and plans, this means the organization relies on an individual's judgement to guide organization operations.

b) An organization without qualified finance staff will eventually start to have difficulties managing or attracting donor funds. The organization runs the risk of closure due to debts incurred.

c) An organization without HR policies or a clear organization structure does not effectively attract, motivate and retain competant staff who are crucial towards the achievement of an organization's objectives.

d) The lack of a clear organization's strategic document means organizations are easily manipulated by other stakeholders or are not able to clearly source for funds to support their interventions.

e) The technical competence of the organization in the identified project is crucial. If this lacks, then the organization's programmatic competence is questionable and performance is compromised.

f) Many organizations' survival rate are low as they are unable to get the right people on board or retain them for extended periods due to weak or inadequate management systems. The growth and retention of innovative staff and the availability of funding determines the survival of an entity.

g) Inadequate resource mobilization capacities and focus affects the organization's capacity to have diverse resources and this means they lack protection against shifting donor trends.

h) As NGOs move through its lifecycle phases, boards, which display certain weakness, may eventually create barriers that hinder growth within an NGO and this may limit its organizational capacity. The above consequences can affect an organization's sustainability and causes many local NGOs to close shop after operating for a while.

Individual philanthropists, financial institutions, donor and government agencies are looking for NGOs that are legitimate, accountable, sustainable and transparent. These characteristics can be built through proactive engagement in OD interventions at an organizational level.

Chapter Four: Designing OD interventions

The capacity for sustainable activity and continuity is linked to internal management. This eventually enables organizations manage the environment in which they operate.

While undertaking capacity development to only focus on the technical aspects among staff is not enough. It has become crucial to address organizational issues by building the internal management capacity of the organization.

Before embarking on designing OD interventions there is need to understand the following:

a) HOW does the entity work? How big is the organization and when did it begin operating? Are all parties ready and equipped to support the process? This helps to get the SCOPE and depth of the engagement?

b) WHOSE capacity are you trying to build? At what level will you build capacity? Is it at the individual or organizational level or both. This helps with the target focus.

71

c) The capacity to be built is for WHAT and WHY. This helps determine the purpose or objective.

d) HOW will the change occur?

e) The TIME frame when the interventions need to be undertaken and the COST?

f) WHO will deliver the OD interventions? Internal staff or use external consultants

There is also the need to identify which level to focus on in addition to the above:

a) Organizational level intervention (Systems, Human resource, and Structures)

b) Institutional level intervention (external-policy focus)

c) Individual level(attitudes, skills and knowledge)

d) Or a combination of the above.

In some context to achieve the desired result, it will require interventions at both individual as well as organizational level. An organization development intervention is a progression of, tasks and activities aimed at assisting an entity to boost its execution and potency.

OD interventions intentionally disrupt the status quo; they are conscious steps to restructure an organization toward a different and more functional state. In OD, an effective intervention meets the following criteria:

a) It is aligned to the context and needs of the entity. It has to be relevant to the entity's identified gap.

b) It has its foundation on addressing the cause- effect of a situation and identification of measurable outcomes.

c) Members of the entity have the knowledge and skills to undertake any proposed changes.(Increase change management competence)

Designing effective interventions is affected by the OD practitioner's skills and abilities, attitudes and perceptions of individual members of the organizations, organizational and cultural factors and the focus where change is targeted to occur. Changing the rules that are in existence in organizations is often challenging and even more so when the rules are informal in nature. Hence, there is a need for clear understanding of the components that define an organization and diverse stakeholders within the organization and their characteristics.

To enable one understand this, an assessment becomes key in selecting a relevant OD intervention. An assessment helps to avoid development of premature and unsustainable interventions. An assessment needs to be thorough however, it is sometimes important to have an initial understanding of the context before engaging in a more detailed approach.

The OD Assessment Process

Before embarking on designing an OD intervention, it is crucial to measure the NGO's current requirements, possessions, as well as its preparedness to tackle internal changes that may be required. An assessment activity serves four purposes:

1. It explores opportunities and gaps within the organization

2. It serves as a collective learning opportunity and creates awareness on the phase of development an NGO is at.

3. It assists in defining and structuring the interventions to be undertaken

4. Helps identify a baseline from which to measure any change or progress.

In instances where the exercise is conducted well it serves as a learning process for both the facilitator and members of the organization.

Different organizations use different approaches and tools when conducting assessments. The key thing to keep in mind is that whichever approach that is used the exercise needs to be undertaken in a participatory and interactive way and should not be linked to funding so that an organization gets to learn from the process.

The use of multi-disciplinary approaches and tools is also highly encouraged and having a team of two to three facilitators depending on the size and number of people within the selected organization. This assists in capturing the perceptions and thoughts of the participants from different perspectives.

The purpose of the OD exercise is to explore the organization's current success, gaps and identify action to address them. The process can be undertaken using the following steps:

1. Get buy-in from management(Contracting stage)

2. Collection of information from documents and individuals using a developed tool to gather perspectives (Preliminary diagnosis)

3. Feedback on data collected and team discussions on explored themes and discussion on possible options to address the gaps identified.(Joint diagnosis)

4. Selection and ranking of priority gaps and joint preparation of the plan of action with team.

5. Identify change champions who will oversee implementation and review of selected priorities

6. Implementation and evaluation of progress

7. Terminate the OD relationship/engagement

It is important to assess progress and identify any barriers that are hindering progress. The action plan is then updated through either replanning or readjusting the priority. It is also worthwhile to note that within any organization there exists a culture (underlying tacit beliefs and values) that will either be visible or not. This can impact on the individual or an organization's capability to participate in the OD process.

Organizational cultures are sometimes deeply ingrained in an organization and they require time for them to be changed. Teams create culture and therefore it is encouraged to use data from focus group discussions to supplement with individual assessments to help understand and identify the prevailing culture within the organization and get consensus on areas for change.

OD practitioners and other scholars have developed a wide variety of assessment tools that can be used to conduct assessments. It is important for an OD practitioner or an organization to select the right and appropriate methodology to conduct an assessment based on the context, size and age of the organization and the purpose for the assessment.

Challenges that Exist in Designing OD Support for NGOs

There are several obstacles experienced when engaging with organizations that in my experience caused barriers in providing the required OD support within various NGOs.

1. **Assessment fatigue**

Many organizations face fatigue because of participating in several assessments and yet no support is provided to help them address the needs identified. This causes dissatisfaction among members of the organizations.

As a facilitator, I have observed that, some organizations undertake upto three assessments conducted by different stakeholders with no feedback or support given to address the gaps identified. This leads to some NGOs members feeling that assessments are a waste of time and do not add any value to the organization.

2. **Fear of losing funding due to the outcome of an assessment**

Organizations are sometimes reluctant to undergo an assessment for fear that this will affect the funding they would receive. This results in many NGOs postponing the exercise or showing hostility towards the officers supporting the exercise. In some instances they may delay the engagement of an OD exercise for upto six months or one year.

3. Lack of ownership by the organization

When planned actions are undertaken in an unenthusiastic manner, then it is unlikely that the process will produce lasting change compared to those fully supported by the organization involved. While organizations have employees who are committed "activists", they have been reluctant to focus on management issues of the organization.

The reason being that NGOs have a 'culture of action' in which leaders and staff are reluctant to engage significant amounts of time to improve organizational issues, because such a focus will affect the action of 'getting out and doing something'.

4. Focus of the organization's strategy

Many organizations strategies tend to focus more on service provision to 'poor' communities or 'vulnerable groups' through providing support on a short term period. Many lack strategies that target building the organization's sustainability in terms of its internal structures.

There are conflicts between program implementation and building the internal structure. In most cases, program implementation is given priority and included within the organizational strategy but not improving the internal management operations.

5. Low levels of commitment among leaders

Board members and management are not easily available to be part of the initial OD assessment meetings. This makes it difficult for the teams present during the exercise to own the action plan or priority interventions.

Any proposed changes would only be undertaken when the team received a go ahead from both the management team or the board as they provide the overall leadership in the organizations.

6. Size of organization and staffing

The size of the organization and staffing tends to affect the type and frequency of support to be provided. If the organization is small one can only focus on incremental OD support that is not too complex and expensive for the organization.

High staff turnover among the organizations also affects the consistency of support to be given to an organization. Retention of key staff is low in many local NGOs as they are more project-oriented and depend largely on donor funds that support the recruitment of staff.

This presents a challenge, for example, some NGOs would lack a director or project coordinator for over a year due to lack of adequate funds to support the position. This slowed implementation of OD interventions identified.

In most local NGOs, about 75%-80% of the staff are volunteers and not full time employees. This limits the support that can be consistently provided to such organizations, as OD interventions undertaken are not sustained over time due to staff exiting from the organization.

7. **Minimal or no funding to support OD interventions**

Some OD interventions require funds for them to be implemented for example engaging a consultant to help develop a strategic plan or organizational policies. Few donors provide funds for this and it becomes difficult for the organizations to make the required changes. However, overreliance on donor funds can stunt or undermine the NGO's ability to address gaps identified during assessments.

8. **Project mentality focus**

This perspective is encouraged by the practices of donors who focus on activities at project or department level. Project funding in most instances is inflexible and produces uncertainties, which lead to delays in implementation.

This mentality makes members of the organization not to realize how the lack of proper internal structures or lack of capacity within an organization can affect their performance.

9. Inaccessibility of NGOs working in unstable environments

It is a challenge to consistently work or support organizations in conflict zones. Many times conducting the assessments or providing support has to be postphoned or suspended due to conflict and tension in the surrounding environment.

10. Lack of a clear framework for OD support

The focus of the donor supporting capacity development has also has an impact on the extent of and frequency support provided to the local NGO. Many good intentions for support to organizations have been hampered by the lack of a clear focus by the donor agency or stakeholder providing support.

Unless the organization providing OD support is committed and has a clear framework for designing and supporting OD interventions, many of the efforts in OD end at the assessment stage.

Lack of a clear organizational framework also poses a danger because interventions being designed tend to focus more on training or in other instances OD interventions are carried out in an inconsistent manner that eventually does not yield the intended results.

Conclusion:

Unfortunately many stakeholders (for example, donor, government, business agencies) currently concentrate more on building the technical capacity of the staff. This is because many organizations perceive that capacity development interventions on the lower end of the hierarchy (skills development) are more crucial yet this will not change the fundamental patterns in the organization.

One thing the stakeholders fail to understand is that the staff given the technical skills belongs within an organizational setup. Therefore, unless organizational operations are conducive the staff will not put the skills acquired into practice. This justifies the need to improve the internal structures of the organization to enable staff use the skills acquired and eventually the organization's overall performance is improved.

Finally, when designing OD interventions, it is crucial that those being given support own the process and understand the link between performance and internal organization gaps. It is also important when designing OD interventions, to develop consistency and alignment to the organization's strategy, goals and structure.

Chapter Five: Implementation of OD Interventions

For an organization, to thrive and succeed change must be a part of its culture and the entity must have the ability to listen to its environment and evolve accordingly. Loyalty to their essential values should be motivation enough for most NGOs to integrate change and innovation in their everyday operations. Yet this reasoning or perspective is not common in many organizations.

This section will highlight some barriers to the effective implementation of OD interventions and recommend some good practice when supporting organization development within NGOs.

Before embarking on the implementation of OD interventions, it is important to start by asking the following strategic questions.

a) Did the team identify the right PRIORITIES to address the gaps/needs? Are the priorities proposed approved by management? Is the period needed to undertake the actions realistic?

b) Is there a need for a BUDGET for the identified activities?

c) Are the key implementors (ACTORs) on board? Are they available and for what DURATION?

d) Is the team ready for CHANGE? Are there any envisioned barriers? Is there a plan to mitigate the barriers or risks?

e) How will success be determined? What INDICATORs will show success? This helps to develop measurements and indicators for success.

f) How will the TRANSITION phase of the support be carried out? Who will be responsible for initiating the exit? What will necessitate an exit?

If it is noted that for whatever reason an organization is not ready to continue with undertaking implementation of the OD interventions proposed. It would be prudent for the process not to begin to avoid failure and frustrations.

Factors that Hinder Effective Implementation of OD Interventions

There are distinctive characteristics among NGOs that might encourage or slow changes from happening. The following observations are typical of NGOs and may explain their high or low adaptation to change.

1. Low flexibility in the organizational structure

An organization's value clearly shapes its structure and as such is usually less flexible than a business and this slows any process of change. The rigid the structure then the more resistance one is likely to encounter but where the structure is flexible and adaptable then it embraces changes at a faster rate to the advantage of the organization.

2. Emotional connection to the organization

The presence of people with a high emotional connection to the organization or project they are working on is a common feature of many NGOs. People with an emotional connection may have difficulty in seeing where former ways of thinking or planning are no longer effective and need to be changed.

Organizations that do not renew their personnel, particularly in areas requiring leadership run the risk of becoming stagnated by the excessive protection of the organization and overlooking an ever-changing environment. These organizations are unable to detect the need for change.

3. Culture of participation

The culture of participation is without a doubt a feature of many organizations in the sector. Numerous NGOs consider participation as an important value to protect.

It is not unusual to find significant crises related to the process of professionalizing management or organizational growth that are linked to defending a participatory culture, or further still to the tradition of assembly. The culture of participation is strongly related to the way organizations are created.

4. Culture of consensus

Given the characteristics of NGOs, achieving the full consensus of all members is incredibly complex and yet there are many organizations where this culture is deeply rooted. Conflict is perceived as an attack on the very pillars of the organization and as such is ignored or its existence not accepted.

5. Founder syndrome

Local NGOs sometimes face resistance to change from founders of the organizations. The founders are more likely to fail to see the need for change, even where they recognize that it is inevitable if the organization is to progress.

This can be due to a high level of emotional attachment, which delays change when the same individuals show opposition. A failure to understand the reasons for the change, or seeing the change as a threat to the very core of an organization can generate very strong reactions of resistance among founders.

6. Diversity of stakeholders

The variety of stakeholders for example founders, governors, members, donors, workers, volunteers, beneficiaries that exist in an organization also has an impact. The number of stakeholders involved becomes a source of conflict and clearly makes reaching consensus in any process of change difficult.

This is due to their numerous roles and levels of dedication but more so to their will to participate in the key decisions made within the organization. This is often reflected by the lack of objectives which is accompanied by a characteristic emotional attachment to the project.

7. Lack of buy-in from leadership/management

The cost of making change can be incredibly high as leaders perceive that their position in the organization and relationship with the teams will be transformed and they will have "less control".

Leading a process of change requires a firm attitude that is often lacking in many of the leaders and this slows implementation. The leadership style within an organization also affects internal transformation, as decisions must be made to instigate a change in the organization, which is more often at the discretion of the leader.

8. Unclear roles between management and governing bodies

The confusion of roles between the governing bodies and management is a common defect of many NGOs. In small, less professionally structured organizations governing bodies tend to be involved in the daily operations of the organization, exercising strategic leadership and part of operational management.

When the organization is in its initial stages, it may be common for the governing body to be involved in management (and quite often necessary) and clearly contributes to its dynamics. However, in the long term this is not a sustainable practice.

Ideally, the management team should be running the daily operations of the organization under the supervision of the board.

9. Minimal or Scarce resources

Many NGOs have limited resources compared to the volume of activities undertaken. They may detect new needs in one of its markets, but then are required to convince the donors to assist them in addressing the need and adapting the work of the organization.

However, heavy reliance on donors' resources can often delay an organization's goal or need to adapt to the changing environment or community needs. This financial dependence on certain donors may mean that an NGO gradually becomes less daring or innovative.

10. Politically active culture

The organization focus is on action rather than the reflection process. This notion is based on the idea that NGOs were created to provide a solution to an outstanding need that is considered urgent hence, time, effort and resources available are dedicated to what is perceived as the basic mission of the organization.

In smaller organizations, the politically active culture is usually quite apparent. An organization that has limited resources may not detect any need for internal management changes, or if identified, may suffer from the lack of will or ability to make any reflection on its management.

11. Delay in review and approval of policies and documents

In most organizations the approval of policies and tools by management/board would take a long time. This makes it difficult to assess the impact and appropriateness of documents developed.

In some instances it takes for example one –two years for the Board and management to review and approve policies to be used. Without a policy being reviewed or approved institutionalization of the policy becomes difficult.

12. Inadequate mechanisms to evaluate the impact of OD interventions

The absence of a clear system for monitoring and evaluating the impact of OD interventions is a challenge. With the exception of the information sometimes requested by its financiers, the control, monitoring and evaluation of OD interventions has never been a priority in many organizations.

Secondly, challenges of assessing impact of OD interventions arise due to an interchange of factors within and external to the organization, dynamic work environment, and challenges of attribution.

Finally, the culture of many NGOs and their leadership or management styles do not embrace the need for Monitoring, evaluation, reporting and learning (MERL) processes.

Highlights of Good Practice to Improve Uptake of Organization Development Interventions

It is important for OD facilitators to understand that change may occur with individual or organizational behavior. The following are some learning that can promote effective engagement when providing OD support based on the author's experience working with NGOs and materials from selected literature.

1) Understanding the entire organization

In the previous section, the 'three-circle' model emphasized that an organizational change program needs to recognize the nature of an organization and that change in one component has an impact on other aspects.

Change has a holistic dimension (socio-cultural, political, personal, and technical) and it is important to realize that organizational change is not only a technical activity. During implementation of OD interventions, there is need to factor in people and their feelings, values, beliefs and the cultural and political realities of any organization. If change is looked at as a technical exercise only and the other components are ignored, it is unlikely to have much lasting outcome.

2) Acknowledge and strengthen the existing strengths

When conducting the diagnosis one realizes that the organization has some strength that can be used as a positive force to encourage changes. This ensures the organization is not overwhelmed by many proposed internal changes at once.

It is also important to note that different organizations have different capacities and that they have within them strengths that can be harnessed further to have a multiplier effect in other areas. The use of appreciative inquiry methodologies is highly recommended and helps build ownership among the teams.

3) Creating a sense of urgency on the need to change

The determining factor of success for an OD intervention is that the organization owns the process of change. The organization must realize the benefit of the change and envision how the organization would be, once the change is finally implemented.

4) Leadership support and commitment

The extent of commitment to undertake a change process is closely linked with the style of leadership support that exists within an organization. Unless the leadership is committed to supporting change then any effort made is doomed to fail. There is a link between the commitment of an organization to undertake OD interventions and its leadership support.

Leadership must be the driving force behind embracing the effort to change. Leadership can demonstrate commitment by incorporating the assessment results and OD interventions into the planning and budgeting process for the organization. On the other hand, an NGO leadership can show commitment by providing funding to assist in undertaking a capacity building intervention.

5) Strengthen governance structures

Many capacity-building efforts among local NGOs focus mostly on building the competencies of project teams and management, but organizational boards are unfortunately not targeted. The area of board governance strengthening is rarely addressed in many capacity development initiatives at the local NGO level.

Yet if the governance structure or competence of an organization is not built then efforts at the lower level in the organization will have no impact or change. Where there is a strong board representation, with members who understand the importance of undertaking OD interventions then it is easier to implement and the process tends to take a shorter duration to support.

In many local NGOs, the board members are recruited to adhere to a donor requirement for funding and hence they remain dormant and do not actively participate in the organization's growth.

Many board members invited to participate in the boards do not understand their roles clearly and how they can support the growth of the organization. This then affects their capacity to guide the organization.

Most board members are recruited from diverse backgrounds with minimal or no experience in governance. It is important that boards are assessed if sustainable transformation and growth is to take place within an organization.

6) Commitment and involvement of key stakeholders

The involvement of key staff and board in the implementation of OD priority interventions is critical. The involvement of all is important as OD cuts across different levels and everyone has to participate if the organization is to succeed.

There is a need to identify and engage all the relevant people in the process and get them to participate in diverse ways in the process based on their capacity, position, influence, and creativity.

7) Identify internal change agents /champions

An organization needs to identify and support a task force or group that will drive the OD implementation process internally. However, the team needs support from the leadership to make decisions or, they will become frustrated.

8) Engage skilled OD consultants

It is important for OD practitioners intending to work with organizations to have a clear understanding about the unique issues that the organizations experience. It is important for them to understand how organizations evolve, the culture, perceptions and some barriers to be encountered at different stages.

9) Use an appropriate mix of participatory approaches and tools

Implementation of OD interventions requires adoption and use of a variety of tools and processes that are considered relevant and appropriate to the size, culture, age and context of the organization.

It is important to understand the lifecycle stage that the organization is at and be able to diagnose the needs it faces during that phase and then select the appropriate tools for engagement. For example, the cluster approach has been used in capacity building by some international NGOs and it is yielding good results.

10) Develop and trigger change with care

Organizations are at various phases of growth and capacity and it is important to understand the history and complexity of the organization. This will help minimize frustration caused when implementation takes longer than expected and changes are seen to take awhile.

For example, donors sometimes trigger an organizational change process on the agenda and this has major implications on how changes within the organization are carried out. Such an approach impacts on ownership of the process as to whether it is with the organization or donor who has control over key resources and hence the process runs the risk of being perceived as a donor-imposed change.

11) Develop local OD providers

For OD work to be effective, it often involves long-term mentorship and coaching. Donors and funders need to understand the changing context and think strategically about supporting the development of local capacity. This can include building capacity of existing national NGOs that are involved in OD consultancy services by training OD consultants and /or creating a capacity-building center of excellence or unit.

12) Donor commitment to see the OD process through

Implementation of OD interventions sometimes requires long-term support, which is often perceived as costly in terms of time and money. If a donor decides to support an OD process, it should be committed to supporting the process to the end and not to transition midway leaving the organization with a half-baked process.

The organization that offers support needs to develop a clear strategy on what support will be given, for how long and what outcomes they expect to see so that they can measure the outcomes. This will ensure the commitment to support interventions is consistent and brings added value.

13) Coordinate with other agencies and within departments

Donors supporting OD need to ensure that there is consensus and coordination amongst them. Donors who may not share the same understanding of OD or their role in the process may undermine the OD process.

Sometimes this has lead to confusion in the OD process as each donor uses different approaches and they are not willing to embrace another way of doing things. Secondly, there is a need for coordination and alignment within the donor offering OD support. For example, a department within the donor organization supports a long-term process, while another department focus is on short-term demands; this scenario sends conflicting information to the organization receiving support.

14) Monitoring and reporting of OD progress

It is important to develop objectives and indicators that will assist in monitoring of the OD activity implementation. There is a need to ask what are the results or outcome we need to observe when an intervention has been undertaken and is complete.

Many at times the lack of a clear results framework to guide measuring the progress and impact of an OD intervention means that organizations become comfortable with the first level output of that the intervention once it has been done.

Yet there is a need to go further and explore what changes are seen because of undertaking the OD activity. For example when an HR policy is drafted what difference does it make in the organization, what changes do we need to observe? This entails having a focus on a results-oriented approach to nurturing and building internal organization systems and structures.

Chapter Six: Role of OD in Change Management

Evaluators, governments, NGOs, and donor agencies are raising critical questions about the nature and impact of diverse OD interventions on organizational effectiveness. The aim of OD is to build stronger organizations and use of OD approach will support organizations achieve sustainability and growth in the end.

However, local NGOs must acknowledge and understand OD and the process of change. Management consultants have observed for many years that the core competency of any organization is the capacity to manage and embrace change while still maintaining high-performance standards and not losing focus on the mission of the organization.

Overview of Change in Organizations

Change is an ongoing process that involves deliberation, engagement, and awakening to act. Local NGOs need to understand that there is a need to continually evolve towards effectiveness that aligns with the demands and needs during a specified period.

Due to emerging challenges, opportunities, and interrelationships between various internal and external actors there is a need for organizations to enhance their ability to adapt to change for them to succeed. Organization alignment, adaptation, and learning are therefore critical elements to building an efficient organization.

Woodman, Pasmore, and Shani [xx] argue that for an organization to be effective, leaders are required to re-align an organizational design, culture, and people with continuous changes in the competitive environment.

It seems almost indisputable that the very organizations that were born to make change are actually highly sensitive to any kind of alteration in their internal surroundings. NGOs are normally unprepared to undertake any kind of change as an essential part of their daily existence.

Many NGOs face the challenge of retaining a level of resiliency during processes of change and this continues to be a burden among OD practitioners. This is because some NGOs have taken on "bureaucratic" characteristics, in terms of structure, process, and behavior.

The reality however is that NGOs irrespective of their size, type, longevity, phase of development, geographic area need to be effective in the perspective of the stakeholders around them and those whom they serve if they are to be considered legitimate and effective in their operations.

This then requires organizations to embrace change and learn continuously if they are to evolve and grow. It is people and not organizations that change and when individuals and teams change then the organization changes.

Managing change is about managing individuals and organization's interest, keeping opposition under control and building sustained commitment towards the achievement of the prioritized OD interventions.

It is crucial to engage OD practitioners and capacity builders to assist local NGOs develop structures, and competence to help them undertake organizational and donor mandates. This is because as the development scenario, demands and needs change then what defines or constitutes effectiveness will certainly change.

Understanding the Change Process

It is important to understand the change process at both individual and organizational level. There are different models or frameworks that could help individual and organizations understand the change process.

The Change pyramid

When managing change, there is the need to understand that, the lower pyramid components are visible and easier to address (these are elements like tasks, roles, and structure). As one moves higher towards the peak of the pyramid (elements like behavior and culture), change at this level becomes difficult, as these traits are mostly invisible and the level of discomfort increases.

In many organizations it is easy to assume that once the lower level components are addressed then change has occurred however if the other elements in the other two components are not addressed then the organization will see no differences in the interventions implemented.

The model advocates for tackling the lower component of the pyramid thereby introducing gradual changes especially where there is resistance or fear of change. This will help the organization appreciate the change process and realize quick wins.

The modification of strategies, structures, or systems is often necessary, but it goes beyond this; for a change to really prevail, it must lead to a new culture, a shared pattern of behavior and values. If this is not the case, the change will simply survive at the most superficial levels of an organization and sustainability will not be achieved.

Therefore, a change is not complete until it has been institutionalized within the organization, as an integral part of the culture. It is not enough to only spot the leaders of the change and outline strategies to overcome resistance.

Obstacles to change can be found in the very structure or culture of the organization. In other situations resistance comes from middle management level individuals with minimal exposure to change practices.

Therefore, individuals and organizations embarking in the change process need adequate support and it is important to recognize their efforts and offer rewards along the way.

Lewin's Model in change management:

This model has three phases unfreeze, change and lastly refreeze. For example a large cube of ice that needs to be altered or recreated into a cone shape, it will require one to melt the ice (unfreeze) and mold the melted ice water to the desired shape (change you want to see). Finally, solidify the new shape (refreeze).

In unfreezing, the desire is to remove prejudices, barriers that will hinder change from occurring. This needs an understanding of the organization and its structure.

In refreezing new habits and practices are adopted and institutionalized after being identified in the molding phase. Recognizing that change is a process with well-defined stages then, an organization can prepare a blueprint to guide the anticipated changes that are likely to take place.

For an organization to experience practical changes, then it must begin by discerning the reason why a shift must occur. It is important to re-examine beliefs and perceptions held both at the individual and organizational level. Change begins from this unfreezing stage.

Many times many organizations reach the mold stage and disregard the refreeze stage, which is more often the institutionalization of the change. This means employees are left at the transition trap if refreezing does not occur which is a phase of creating stability.

All too often, people go into organizational changes blindly and without the commitment to follow through and this causes unnecessary turmoil within the organization.

Two Significant Motivational Factors for Change

i.   Change to survive

Surviving in a changing environment is a major priority that drives an organization to change. Change can be linked to transformation in the environment, within the organization itself or a crisis that makes it indispensable. The most difficult time to change is when everything seems to be going well and detecting required changes becomes a daunting task.

ii.   Change to increase impact

As well as the basic need for survival, an organization's need to experience impact is a major motivation that leads to change. The capacity for adaptation is an important aspect for an organization to achieve its mission. Organizations with the ability to learn from their experience while continuing to modify any programs or plans will be truly successful.

Resistance to change

Understanding why there is resistance to change is important when undertaking or supporting OD interventions among local NGOs. The following are reasons why some organization may resist change:

1. Defending personal interests

One reason that might lead people to oppose a change is in defense of their own interests. Loss of status, fear of being relegated with the adoption of new circumstances or losing their job or position of power.

2. Lack of understanding and/or trust

A lack of understanding is another reason behind the strongest resistance. It is usually among people who are highly connected to the organization, who reject any changes based on their commitment to an institutional project and their "experience" in the organization.

3. Lack credibility

The lack of credibility or trust in those that are instigating a change is another reason for people to resist or fail to commit to it. A lack of credibility is often explained by the fact that the person instigating change is not legitimate in the organization or does not have the backing of the team or management. Likewise, the organization may have attempted various changes in the past that were unsuccessful.

4. Low tolerance to change

Intolerance among certain people or organizations to change can lead to resistance. A lack of tolerance is connected to actual character; however, it is often the nature of the organizational culture itself. Any previous negative experiences or past failures in attempts to make changes will aggravate the situation even more.

5. Culture

In an organization's development, the culture of an organization can be used as a tool to assist the entity gain victory. Organizations are cultural entities, and to realize desired change it requires a change in culture. If any change is to be experienced in an organization, then culture has to be transformed or adjusted. If there occurs an adjustment in culture and new approaches are embraced as the ideal, then change endures.

Ubels, Naa-Aku, and Fowler[xxi] observe that without changing culture other changes are likely to be short-lived and effectual. They further state that the cultural aspects of any organization exist and operate unconsciously.

Therefore, in due course the organizations develop particular ways of doing things. This particular way of doing things is what sometimes creates resistant to much-needed changes that would see growth within an organization.

Strategies to Overcome Resistance

It is crucial as a development practitioner to identify if there are any stalled change programs in the past or currently before embarking on introducing, any new interventions. This will help in understanding the reasons why changes were not sustained and explore the possibility of reviving the change project if it is still relevant within the context and time period.

However, there are a different mechanisms and strategies that can be engaged to deal with resistance. There is need to consider the level of authority and legitimacy of the resistant person(s) or groups. Other factors to consider are the importance of consensus in the organization and the ability to integrate the resistant person in the change so as to identify the most suitable strategy to follow.

The following are the list of strategies to address resistance.

i.   **Hard strategies**- these include coercion, manipulation, negotiation, and agreement.

ii. **Soft strategies**-these include facilitation, involvement, build capacity through training, communication

Change management is not an easy task and requires time. It means modifying attitude and behaviors and this complex process does not always necessarily work the first time around.

Achieving Change Within Organizations

Achieving change in an organization is not an easy task and should not be viewed as a "quick fix" process that can happen within a short span.

In every change, process within an organization there will be different roles played by various individuals at certain stages. Individuals can play roles like change initiators, change facilitators, change implementers, and change recipients.

When planning for change in organizations the pyramid of organizational change can be used. This framework guides organizations to identify their strengths and gaps, explore areas where changes are needed and helps to identify persons responsible for ensuring the action to realize the change is undertaken.

The framework can be used to appraise the extent of strategic organizational development and the level of success that can be sustained. It is important to note that having a change management plan is only the beginning of the process and all those involved need to be proactive to effect the change action steps.

The following highlights some key steps an organization can adopt to achieve success in the process of change.

a) Generate change

Step 1: Establish a sense of urgency

Step 2: Get commitment and support at management level

Step 3: Form a leadership team that will help monitor the change

Step 4: Create a vision for change

b) Promote change

Step 5: Strategically communicate the vision and strategy.

Step 6: Identify champions to lead others to act on the vision

Step 7: Develop a plan for that will include short-term wins

Step 8: Implement, consolidate improvement and document change

c) Institutionalize change

Step 9: Institutionalize the new approaches

Step 10: Introduce the change in the organizational culture through transformational leadership approach

Step 11: Monitor and review plan based on changes realized

Ideally, organizational leadership needs transforming, mental, and 'softer' skills (empathy and understanding) to create a conducive environment that will support effective change actions.

Overview of Possible Changes to be Observed

Changes are likely to be experienced because Organizational Development interventions target improvement of efficiency and increase the capacity of the organization to implement its mandates.

The following are possible changes that can be observed at organizational level

a) **Organizational Culture**

Changes in individual attitudes, practices, or behavior within the organization

b) **Policy & Standards**

Change in rules or policies that guide an organization's operations.

c) **Process & Systems**

Change in an organization's methods of functioning.

d) **Organizational Strategy**

Change or revisions in the course of the mission and vision as a result of changes experienced in the external environment

e) **Structure**

Change in the way an entity repositions itself to realize its objectives.

f) **Collaboration and Alliances**

Changes in the way entities work with other organizations and stakeholders.

g) **Learning and Innovation**

The acquisition and development of new skills, knowledge, and ideas.

h) **Technology**

These are changes realized in the way technology is used or technology that is adopted to ease operations within the organization.

Strategies to Assist Local NGOs Sustain Change

Making progress in pre-planned changes, motivating commitment of teams, and minimizing or removing organizational obstacles that prevent change are important factors to consider but not sufficient to believe that a significant change has occurred.

In many local NGOs that are successful in initiating change, they face the dilemma of ensuring the change is sustained. Beckhard and Harris,[xxii] propose the following recommendations to sustain change:

i.   Periodic meetings to share results and perspectives on progress.

ii.   Organization sensing meetings these are important especially where large-scale organizational changes have

123

taken place. Discussions are held to understand whether changes implemented are working and its impact.

iii. Periodic intergroup meetings, these are good especially where the changes are being implemented at a group level.

iv. Renewal conferences, this can involve organizational leaders, board, and staff meeting to evaluate the plan or strategy for change.

v. Goal directed performance reviews, these are linked to the priority actions identified and individuals and teams are evaluated against specific measurable goals.

vi. Periodic visits/revisits from external consultants or change agent, this is a good practice as it can help the organization be objective in reviewing its progress overtime. This helps the leadership of an organization to be accountable for the commitments they made to effect changes within the organization.

vii. Rewards for organizational team members: These are important if change is to be sustained. Recognition, compensation, or promotions are good especially to those teams /members who maintain new and innovative ways of doing things.

Local NGOs are created to achieve some purpose and a choice of strategy has an implication on internal organization characteristics. The growth of an NGO is not always smooth and for an organization to maximize performance, it requires the capacity to structure and restructure itself to adapt to changing internal and external conditions.

The purpose of embracing change should be to develop organizations that can learn how to adapt to internal or external pressures they face at certain times in its growth and existence.

Local NGO leadership should be cautious of perceiving that they can create a "stable" organization in an environment that is constantly changing. Many at times once an organization has "achieved" a desired change the leadership and staff assume that they have accomplished the journey.

According to Anderson,[xxiii] the objective should be to develop practices that support the desired direction and remove barriers to change, and to implement opportunities for regular evaluation and renewal that encourage appropriate and necessary alterations but avoid stagnation.

Therefore, three important aspects are required if changes caused by OD interventions are to be sustained; the existence of clear drivers of change, existence of a plausible change process and a defined vision about the future.

Chapter Seven: Trends and Perspectives in OD

Despite the fact that OD is a powerful tool or approach that can change and influence management of organizations. Many critical questions face the future of organization development (OD) as a development approach. The following areas continue to influence and are influenced by organizational development practices:

OD and Human Resource Management

In future, it will be important for human resource managers to take lead in organizational change activities. This change means that the HR's mandate will expand to include aspects of OD processes to deliver organizational effectiveness.

Human Resource (HR) and Organization development disciplines have certain common elements through utilizing a systems approach, HR and OD practitioners can support together an organization's pursuit to sustainable performance.

HR professionals will need to embrace OD practice because it can play an important strategic role and can influence an organization's culture and contribute towards sustainable changes within organizations.

Using OD to Enhance a Culture of Peer Learning

Failure to create continuously adaptive organizations leads to decline or death of organizations. Assessments undertaken within organizations are good learning experiences if done in a highly interactive environment.

In my view, organizational development processes, like planning and organizing should be seen as learning opportunities that could contribute to an organization's growth.

Peer learning among NGOs can be encouraged by using the cluster approach, which is useful where several organizations exist in a region. It is a development approach that maybe worthwhile while undertaking OD interventions. This method has been used in other programmatic areas and has been quite successful.

Aligning Organization Strategy and Organization Development

Strategic planning is a process of documenting intentions expressed in the form of a plan. The plan then turns the proposed options into reality by looking at organization's future in relation to the analysis of its immediate environment. A strategic plan that incorporates OD elements enables an organization harness employees' skills and abilities to promote the achievement of its goals.

The prevailing notion is that OD comprises of a group of consultants processing assessments for the purposes of funding an agency. However, OD is an important component that creates a whole system change in terms of organization design and culture change which eventually enhances an organization's performance.

There is a great need for management to understand the role OD plays in an organization and align it to its strategy so as to create organizational value. OD intervention processes that are not aligned or factored in the organization strategy and spending means it is not given priority.

Use of OD Approaches to Manage Alliances

What factors make an alliance or partnership succeed or fail? NGOs both at local and international level are consciously developing strategies to collaborate or merge with other organizations.

An OD (Organization Development) approach can be used to build the partnership process from initiation to the end. OD practitioners can assess an alliance using to identify both short-term and long-term interventions that are appropriate for the partnership growth.

The action research methodology employed by OD approach serves to identify if an effective planned change process will address the alliance objectives by determining what phase of the alliance will require what intervention or changes.

Moreover, OD methodology is flexible and a number of intervention techniques may be employed during different stages of the alliance process to enhance effectiveness. The classical

OD advocates role clarification, improved communication, and team building as means of building effectiveness.

The end stage of any OD intervention requires an in-depth evaluation of the process, such as the implementation stage where both task and culture are integrated into one entity.

Evaluating OD Intervention Results

Evaluation of OD interventions is still uncommon but is increasingly becoming recognized as crucial to measure the changes observed because of the interventions.

Assessing and measuring change because of OD intervention is still a challenge. Currently quite a number of OD measurements have focused on quantitative indicators and very few on qualitative. An evaluation helps identify the feasibility, implementation gaps, and effectiveness of an intervention and outcomes of the interventions at multiple levels.

OD interventions can be described as activities and the nature of evaluation that focuses on activities is process evaluation. This kind of evaluation helps review and track the implementation of an OD intervention. Here one looks at the type and amount of services undertaken, target, inputs used to undertake the intervention, and challenges encountered.

The process questions would ask

i.   What OD intervention was applied, how and why?

ii.   What inputs were used? Duration or period of engagement?

iii. What kind of challenges were encountered and why? How were they addressed?

What has been observed in actual practice is that current efforts in evaluating focus on the extent to which immediate objectives were met within the project and to some extent others go further and assess the effectiveness of the process of the engagement.

A gap that is noted is that much of the OD intervention activities are rarely linked to long-term organizational performance. Performance is described as the ability of an entity to maintain the staff, approaches, learning, organization set-up, and assets it needs to continuously attain its objectives.

Capacity building for organizational change has structures, procedures, and pointers that measure achievement. However, these elements are not fully defined in the organizational plans or after OD practitioners have completed OD support.

In any OD approach, the focus should include developing capacity (short-term) coupled with improvement in organizational performance (long-term).It is important to measure OD change against a baseline. Determining the baseline measurement is therefore crucial. It is vital to include evaluation from the beginning of the design of a capacity- building intervention plan.

The measurement of the impact of OD work is important to help strengthen interventions to be used in NGOs across diverse development sectors and differences.

Blumenthal[xxiv] identifies three levels of outcomes that make up a logical chain that can be evaluated,

1) Grant outputs—were the immediate objectives of the grant met.

2) Organizational outcomes—did the engagement improve the functioning or performance of the organization?

3) Mission impact—did the engagement allow the organization to more effectively serve its mission?

Blumenthal [xxv] further notes that the grant outputs approach to evaluation is most common among funders with relatively small capacity building programs. This logic offers many benefits as it meets the grant maker's requirement for accountability, ensuring that grant funds are spent as promised and its is cost-effective; as it is based upon, grantee self-reports and will be submitted timely once the grant period ends.

Evaluation models are now emerging and there will be need for building the competency of OD practitioners on this. This will assist them measure the effectiveness of the interventions they use to support different organizations.

However, the following areas remain a concern for OD practitioners as they continue to engage with local NGOs

i. Building a sustainable high-performing organization where leadership takes an active role in change management

ii. Building proactive and empowered organizations using OD interventions

iii. Promotion of organizational climate built on continuous learning within an organization.

Conclusion

Building the internal capacity of local NGOs is not a simple task. There exist uncertainties, opportunities, and risks that have an impact on organization's performance that entail flexible and continuous change.

If an organization is not well structured or managed to navigate through the different elements, then its internal management structure and systems gradually weaken. However identifying and designing an organization capacity building program in OD is not always a clear- cut process because organizations are diverse and respond differently to internal or external stimuli.

This means OD programs need to be flexible and customized to suit an organization's character and culture. Yet in addition to that, an organization's internal capacity to adapt and continuously desire to grow contributes to it benefitting from any OD support.

However, for local NGOs to mobilize funding or support for OD interventions, there is need to demonstrate that OD does build sustainable and productive organizations. This can only happen where there is a proactive increase in the uptake and commitment towards implementation of OD interventions.

This can be strengthened further by ensuring there is clear documentation on the changes realized as a result of the OD interventions implemented at organizational level. There is the need to continuously build the knowledge base for OD practitioners and students of development through documentation of the impact of OD interventions as it pertains to local NGOs.

End Notes

[i] Batti Rehema, (2014) Enhancing Non-Governmental Organization capacity through organization development"

http://iiste.org/Journals/index.php/DCS/article/view/12206>.

[ii] Ibid(2014)

[iii] Woodman Richard, Pasmore William, Shani Abraham (2011) Research in Organization Change and Development. Bingley, UK: Emerald e-book collection, Ipswich; MA retrieved 2/2/2014

[iv] Blumenthal, Barbara (2001), "How Can We Help?" A Comparison of Capacity Building Programs" Research paper. *foundationcenter.org/gainknowledge/…/practicematters_07_paper.pdf*

[v] Acquaye-Baddo, Ubels Naa-Aku, Fowler Alan,(2010) Capacity Development in Practice. London. Earthscan

[vi] Ibid (2010)Pg 18-20

[vii] Ibid (2010)Pg146

[viii] Ibid (2010)Pg 206

[ix] Batti Rehema, (2014) Enhancing Non-Governmental…

[x] Sahley, C. (1995) 'Strengthening the capacity of NGOs: cases of small enterprise development agencies in Africa', INTRAC Management and Policy Series no. 4,Oxford: International NGO Training and Research Centre.

[xi] Blumenthal, Barbara. (2001).

[xii] Ibid (2001)

[xiii] Woodman, Pasmore and Shani (2011)Pg 4

[xiv] Ibid (2011)Pg 57

[xv] Anderson Donald,(2012) Organization Development: The process of leading organizational change. Los Angeles. SAGE publications

[xvi] Code Of Ethics,(2009) CCIC-CCCI. (n.d.). Retrieved from http://www.ccic.ca/_files/en/what_we_do/002_ethics_march_chart_code.pdf

[xvii] Daft Richard, Hugh Willmot, Jonathan Murphy (2010), Organization theory and design, p. 356 Singapore: Cengage Learning Inc.

[xviii] Batti Rehema (2014) Human resource management challenges facing local NGOs. Retrieved from http://article.sciencepublishinggroup.com/pdf/10.11648.j.hss.20140204.11.pdf

[xix] Batti Rehema (2014) Challenges facing local NGOs in resource mobilization. Retrieved on 31.3.2015 from http://article.sciencepublishinggroup.com/pdf/10.11648.j.hss.20140203.12.pdf

[xx] Woodman, Pasmore, Shani,(2011). Page 14

[xxi] Acquaye-Baddo, Ubels N Fowler Alan, (2010)

[xxii] Beckhard, R and Harris R,(1977) Organizational transitions. Reading, MA: Addison-Wesley

[xxiii] Donald A(2012)

[xxiv] Blumenthal, Barbara, (2001)

[xxv] Ibid (2001)

Printed in Great Britain
by Amazon